COST OF LIVING

BY
MARTYNA MAJOK

★

★

DRAMATISTS
PLAY SERVICE
INC.

The world premiere of COST OF LIVING was produced by the Williamstown Theatre Festival (Mandy Greenfield, Artistic Director; Michael Sag, General Manager) in July 2016. It was directed by Jo Bonney, the scenic design was by Wilson Chin, the costume design was by Jessica Pabst, the lighting design was by Jeff Croiter, the sound design was by Ben Truppin-Brown, the original music was by Justine Bowe, the movement consultant was Thomas Schall, and the production stage manager was David H. Lurie. The cast was as follows:

EDDIE .... Wendell Pierce
ANI .... Katy Sullivan
JESS .... Rebecca Naomi Jones
JOHN .... Gregg Mozgala

COST OF LIVING was originally produced Off-Broadway by Manhattan Theater Club (Lynne Meadow, Artistic Director; Barry Grove, Executive Director), in association with the Williamstown Theatre Festival, opening on June 7, 2017. It was directed by Jo Bonney, the scenic design was by Wilson Chin, the costume design was by Jessica Pabst, the lighting design was by Jeff Croiter, the original music and sound design were by Robert Kaplowitz, and the movement consultant was Thomas Schall. The cast was as follows:

EDDIE .... Victor Williams
ANI .... Katy Sullivan
JESS .... Jolly Abraham
JOHN .... Gregg Mozgala

FOLKS

EDDIE. late 40s. male.

ANI. early 40s. female. pronounced "Ah-nee."

JESS. mid 20s. female.

JOHN. mid 20s. male.

PLACE

The urban east of America. Jersey.
The near present.

The prologue, scenes seven, eight, and nine occur on the same Friday night in December, a week before Christmas. The rest of the play spans the months of September through December.

DIALOGISTICS

Slashes // indicate overlap.
Ellipses ... are active silences.
[Square brackets] are words intended but unspoken.
(Non-italicized parentheticals) within dialogue are meant to be spoken.

A NOTE ON JOHN'S LANGUAGE

John has a speech pattern that manifests itself in a kind of halted way of speaking. This is due to the vocal tension of his cerebral palsy. The breaks and spacing in his lines are meant to simulate that halting rather than to indicate any sort of poetic recitation.

SOME NOTES ON PERFORMANCE

Self-pity has little currency in these characters' worlds. Humor, however, has much.

For the Jersey mouth, the word "fuckin" is often used as a comma, or as a vocalized pause, akin to the word "like." ["I can't like, decide, y'know." = "I can't fuckin, decide, y'know."] It's a word with extra purpose. It's not necessarily *just* a container for anger.

A NOTE ON CASTING

Please cast disabled actors in the roles of John and Ani.

Please assemble a cast that looks like North Jersey and its beautiful diversity. In the prologue, Ani's full name can be Ania Lucja Skowronska-Torres or Ani Luz Hernandez-Torres or Ani Li-Torres or Ānanda Singh-Torres, amongst many options. Ani's full name should be chosen to suit the actress playing her. Also in the prologue, *Na zdrowie* can be replaced with *Salud*, or في صحتك, or 건배, etc., to suit the actress playing Ani. In scene eight, the phone call should be translated into a non-English language to suit the actress playing Jess.

"And I believe I can do this in an ordinary kitchen with an ordinary woman and five eggs... She and I and the kitchen have become extraordinary; we are not simply eating; we are pausing in the [lonely] march [of living] to perform an act together, we are in love; and the meal offered and received is a sacrament which says: I know you will die; I am sharing food with you; it is all I can do, and it is everything."

—Andre Dubus, "Broken Vessels"

"There's something about taking the cart back instead of leaving it in the parking lot. It's significant. Because somebody has to take them in. And if you know that, and you do it for that one guy, you do something else. You join the world. You move out of your isolation and become universal."

—Andre Dubus, "Dancing After Hours"

"Czemu tak się rozsypujemy? Człowiek to głupio inżynierowany."
"Why do we crumble like this? People are stupidly engineered."

—Paweł Majok

COST OF LIVING

Prologue.

*An empty space. An empty stage. That is, a bar in December.
Specifically, St. Mazie's bar in post-Bloomberg Williamsburg,
Brooklyn.
One might call it a hipster bar.*

*A man. Eddie Torres. An unemployed truck driver. He looks
out of place here.
Eddie Torres is a man who understands that self-pity and
moping are privileges for people who, in their lives, have friends
and family who unconditionally love them and will listen to
their shit. Anything he tells you, he hopes will be entertaining
or funny or interesting because he knows you're not obligated
to stay and listen to him. When he slips into sadness, he
bounces back fast. He would have made a great uncle.*

He nurses a glass of seltzer.

EDDIE. The shit that happens is not to be understood.

That's from the Bible.

The shit that happens to you is Not To Be Understood.

So, see, this fucked me up a little when one day comes this call from
Columbia Presbyterian. Is this Mister Torres? There's been a compli-
cation. I'm 49 and I've done nothin but love the fuck outta this woman
for two decades and a year almost. Nothin. Who deserves that?

And a week from her birthday. Seven days.

We were gonna go to Maine. For her birthday.

See the trees.

I leave the lights on now, every room.
Smoke signal: I'm still here.

Holidays are hard.
Christmas next week—that's gonna be hard.

But listen to me holy shit the GLOOM. Get a drink. On me. Made a promise to myself. A penalty. I start talkin gloom, I get it in the WALLET. Lemme buy you a drink. What do you want? Order what you want, I'm payin. This place is my fuckin SWEAR jar.

Order what you want. Go ahead.

Me myself personally, I'm off it. That first day you wake up to find you are *not* in a pool of some kinda liquid, my friend? Vomit, say, or piss? That day? That day is a beautiful fuckin gift upon yer life, man. You are grateful for that day. And you are ready.

That day's the day it's all gonna change.

Signs are real.

This I know cuz I used to drive trucks. Cross-country. Loved it. Loved every aspect of the job. The scenery. Every aspect. The fuckin *scenery*. Utah? Jesus H, man. Utah's gorgeous and no one even knows!

But then I got popped for a DUI. In a car. Blocks from home.
Lost my CDL.
Shit's Creek.
So I got the memories. And some unemployment.

That life is good for people. I was thankful for every day they ain't invented yet the trucker-robots.
That life is good. The road. Sky. The scenery.
Except the loneliness.
Except in the case of all the, y'know, loneliness.
This was what my wife was good for.
Not that this was the only thing.
But everyone what's married there's, y'know, the *fuuuuck* days. Like, *fuuuuck* what did I do. What did I actually fuckin do here.

Cuz, y'know, you married a *person*. And a person's gonna be a person even if they're married.
That's a lesson. That's a lesson for yer LIFE right there.

But still I
I still

still loved her.

She would text me. On the road.
At night. In motels.
Which, alone, can be, can drum up certain feelings.
This is why there's Bibles in motels.
We're all of us, in motels, on the road to somewhere we ain't at yet and that makes us feel feelings.
Roads are dark and America's long.

And I mean this wasn't *poetry*, these texts.
This wasn't like, y'know… *(Tries to remember a verse of a poem, can't.)* …poetry.

"Thinkin Of You."

"How's Things."

"Yer check came today."

"Off to bed."

"Good night."

That little buzz in my pocket or on the nightstand, that's the rope gets tossed down to you at the bottom of that well. When the thoughts come. Y'know. The Thoughts. That loneliness. The texts, they're like, climb on up outta there, y'know. Get up outta those thoughts, y'know, cuz "Thinkin Of You."

Truckers got wild imaginations.
Lots of time to think.
Just not much time to do much with all we been thinkin
except what don't take time at all.
And what's cheap.

(Toasts.) Salud.
(Remembers, re-toasts.) Na zdrowie. * She taught me that.
     Sips his drink.

And sleep. And we sleep.
If we can.

So I started
textin her.
After she
passed.
Like every few days.
"Thinkin Of You."

"Off to bed."

"Hope yer well."

   …

"Miss you."

I'd lie a little too.

"Job hunt's goin good."

And joke.

"My love to Jesus."

"Slip in a good word."

   …

"What are you wearing."

It was nice.

To talk.
To think of her, I mean.
It was just a nice thing that happened.

I owe you another, by the way. For the gloom.
     Tries to change the subject/mood.

---

* Pronounced [naz drove-yeah]. See note on casting.

So I was hopin that, for like community service, they'd gimme a gig that was around people. Like bringin food to old people or like, bein in plays. Walkin puppies, somethin like that. Brushin cats. But I'm painting fences in Livingston. Humane Society's full up. So now my phone's got all this paint and shit on it now, on the cover. "Thinkin of you."

...

I prolly shouldn't be here. At uh, at St. Mazie's here. In uh, in Williamsburg here. All you young people here. With yer fashions. With yer... Pabst.

Prolly shouldn't be here.

Sips his drink.

This is seltzer, this.

For now.

It's maybe not good for me, right now, to be here.
Too close, y'know how sometimes you get so close? You just get a little too close? Moths, man. Like a moth. I know I shouldn't be here but I'm, tonight I'm, I'm comin home from paintin fences, right? Take the train. Bus. Walk. I'm home. Shower. Eat. Like usual now. Alone. And I'm sittin in my house, my apartment, my home, and I'm lookin at the boxes. All the boxes. Of her stuff. And I'm thinkin how this was her mug. Her bowl she liked. The chair. And I'm tempted. Not gonna lie. I'm tempted as all fuckin fuck. Not even 7 yet. Places will be open. Stores. And, even if they're not, then bars. I can do whatever I want. I remember I can do what I want cuz why not, actually. Actually, why the fuck not.

And that's when the phone buzzes.
On the table.

I didn't scream.
But shit I jumped.

...

"Thinkin of you

13

too."

...

I may or may not have pissed myself at that moment.

It's my wife.

It's comin from my wife.

Her number.

Her number

My wife!

Fuckin, fuckin Ani! Ania Lucja Skowronska-Torres!* My wife!!

And then I realize
I realize
her number
they gave away her number.

She's officially gone.

...

And I'm straight up tempted right then.
Why not.
It's not even 7.
Why not.

Buzz.

Thing buzzes again.

"Where are you?"

I wonder how long this person's got my messages for. I wonder if I should be embarrassed. I sent her a picture one time. *(Not that kinda picture, buddy.)* Of a fence I painted.
I don't remember everything I said.

Buzz.

---

* Pronounced [anya loots-ya skov-ron-ska]. See note on casting.

14

"I'm at St. Mazie's."

This is not my wife this is not my wife I know cuz *cmon* this is not my wife I wanna make that clear to you that I don't think this.

But

In that moment?

In that moment, I was comforted to know she's with the good guys.
With St. Mazie.
And that heaven is Catholic.

Buzz.

"It's a bar."

Buzz.

"In BK."
>*Looks confused.*
The fuck is—?

Buzz.

"Brooklyn."
Thank you.

Buzz.
>*Makes a judgmental face for Williamsburg.*
"Williamsburg."

Buzz.

"You?"
>...
Buzz.
>...
"You?"
>...
It's 7 o'clock in Bayonne. The snow just started fallin.

And I wonder what to do.
This is not my wife this is not Ani my wife.

But

But honestly, I dunno what else to do.
Except I *do*, I do know what else to do.
I always know what else I COULD do.
But maybe
maybe something…
the shit that happens is not to be understood
and so maybe I should get some fuckin pants on and GO.

I'm in a cab (okay my car don't tell nobody).
I'm on the PATH.
I'm on the L. (The L!)
I'm here.

I'm here.

> *He takes in the Williamsburg bar.*

And nobody looks like my wife.

Or at me.

Except you.

Yer
Yer real nice.
Yer a real nice guy, man.
I ain't been buzzed yet, texted, since, so. So maybe whoever it, y'know, she's gone.

Man. A ghost ever stood YOU up, man?

Shit listen to me. The GLOOM. That's number three. Yer killin me here. Get a drink. On me. No no no don't even think about passin, man. I owe you.
My treat.

> *He tries to catch a bartender, who ignores him, passes him by. He looks back at his guest.*

Y'know what though? Whoever it is, was, Miss Mazie Saint Mazie

or whatever this place is, fuckin, I hope she's havin a good night. I say that genuinely, man. Even though she stood me up. The punk. I'm playin. I hope she found someone here and ended up she's havin a real good night right now. Whatever that means to her. I hope she found someone to share the night with. That's important. Seemed like she really needed someone to talk to.
It's important.

Go ahead, man. Drink's on me. Made a promise to myself. A penalty. You get just one more drink for all I put you through. Go ahead, I'm payin.

...

Please?

One.

Early September.
It's raining outside.

An accessible apartment in Princeton. A well-kempt and rich one.

Jess stands alone, a bit nervous. But hiding it. She wears a soaked hoodie and jeans/sweats. First generation child of an immigrant. Does not come from wealth, nor does she try to seem it. Has a hard time keeping her feelings and opinions to herself. Which has gotten her in trouble. Still, she can't help it. Or doesn't want to. She will put up a fight when she needs—and sometimes even when she doesn't or perhaps shouldn't. Can take care of herself. Though perhaps wishes this were not always the case.

It's been a while. And she feels very foreign here.

JESS. Nice apartment.
    No response. She waits.
    She judges his nice apartment.

Should I be—?

JOHN. *(From off.)* Hold on.

JESS. Cuz I could— *[tidy or]*

JOHN. *(From off, "stop talking.")* Can't hear you.

JESS. Is there somethin you want me to do?, while yer—

> *Flush, offstage.*

Cuz I would never take advantage of the hourly rate, if I were hired. Not, y'know, doin anything while yer—in there.

> *John enters in a wheelchair.*
>
> *He is beautiful.*
>
> *John has cerebral palsy.*
> *A kind of halted way of speaking.*
> *Otherwise, he is determinedly polished.*
> *Comes from wealth and wears it, undeniably.*
>
> *Jess had prepared for this. Had prepared to look unfazed.*
> *But she is. She is fazed.*
> *And he is beautiful.*
>
> *He looks her over a while before speaking.*

JOHN. Do you have a problem being alone?

> …

JESS. No.

JOHN. You would get to think a lot. Waiting's part of the job.

JESS. Sorry, I never worked with the, Differently-Abled—

JOHN. Don't do that.

JESS. What?

JOHN. Don't call it that.

JESS. Why, I—

JOHN. Don't call it different
-ly-abled.

JESS. Shit is that not the right term?

JOHN. It's
fucking retarded.

...

JESS. So what do I How do I, *refer* to you?

JOHN. Are you planning on talking about me?

JESS. No.

JOHN. Why not?
I'm very interesting.

...

JESS. *(Re: bathroom.)* So after you, y'know, then would I have to...?

JOHN. Why do you want
this job?

JESS. I thought,
the experience and I—, it'd be a very Meaningful Experience—

JOHN. Why do you want—

JESS. The money.

JOHN. Good.

JESS. And I'd be good at it. I'm responsible.

JOHN. Oh good. So you wouldn't
lose me.
Have you ever washed someone before?

JESS. Yeah.

JOHN. You have?

JESS. Yeah.

JOHN. *(Dubious assessment.)*

JESS. *(Not meek, but clearly not a story she cares to share.)* You need
me to like, describe it?

JOHN. How much can you lift? Think you can
lift me?

145 pounds.

Wet.

JESS. I can lift you.

JOHN. You don't need to
bench-press me. You would help lift me out of my chair, and onto my

shower seat. Then you
wash me. Every morning. My hair. Teeth. Trim my
whiskers, on occasion.
You'd keep me handsome.

> *John reaches a shaky hand out to Jess. She hands him her résumé.*
> *He takes it, with two hands, and unfolds it—possibly partly*
> *with his mouth—and smoothes it out on his thighs. Looks at it.*
> *Judges.*

JESS. Whatever I haven't done, I'd figure it out.

JOHN. And this is all
present employment?

JESS. Yeah.

JOHN. A lot of
present employment.

JESS. *(A quiet dig.)* Fer some people. Yeah.

JOHN. These are late bars?

JESS. What?

JOHN. *(Impatient.)* These are late bars, bars that
stay open late, that you // work at?

JESS. Depends but. Yeah. Yes. They're open late.
(Suddenly realizing.) I understood you It wasn't cuz I couldn't The
way you How you Your um—
Yeah they're open late.

> *John looks back down at the résumé.*

I'd set an alarm.

JOHN. You went here?

JESS. Where?

JOHN. To school. Here.

JESS. Yeah.
I went here. Few years ago. Fer undergrad.

Why wouldn't I.

JOHN. So why are you still here? In
September. At the start of the school year. If you
graduated.

JESS. Fer this job.

JOHN. Interview.

JESS. Fer this job interview.

JOHN. Curious.

JESS. What.

JOHN. That you're here for *this* kind of job.
If you graduated from // Prince—

JESS. I graduated.
With honors.

JOHN. It doesn't say on the—What // did you study—?

JESS. I'm just lookin for a side job. Somethin extra. For on the side.

JOHN. In addition to all the— // cocktail wait—?

JESS. It's a loud as fuck alarm.

    ...

And you?, yer here for... *(Trying to guess his age.)* ... // college?

JOHN. PhD.
Graduate School.
For Political Science. Just moved here.
From *Cambridge*.

        He waits for her to be impressed.
        She's giving him nothing.
        On purpose.

Near Boston.

        Nothing.

...Massachu—

JESS. Harvard.

JOHN. Since you mention it.

        John judges the résumé. Jess gets nervous.

JESS. Listen whatever I haven't done, I'd figure it out—

JOHN. How much life have you lived?

JESS. I'm...25—

JOHN. Numbers don't
interest me. How much life

have you seen?
Not everyone can do this work.

JESS. Why? You make shit hard fer people?

JOHN. This "shit" can, by nature, be hard. Not everyone can
cut it. I don't hire from agencies; so some
applicants think they can do it and then it turns out
they can't.

JESS. How come you don't hire from agencies?

JOHN. I don't have to.

JESS. Why not.

JOHN. I have money. I can basically do
anything I want except the things I
can't.

JESS. What's wrong with agencies?

JOHN. They don't appreciate my lawsuits.

If their people mess up, I can sue them so
agencies limit aides to just
doing the basics.

JESS. …What kinda stuff goes beyond the basics?

JOHN. You ask a lot of // questions.

JESS. What might you be havin me do that's not the basics?

JOHN. Various things. // I don't have a—

JESS. But what would I—

JOHN. If you don't interrupt me—because, you see, it can take me
a minute—
if you don't interrupt me, you'll get
all the information you need.

JESS. Sorry.

JOHN. Forgiven. I don't have a list but things come up. You do
whatever I need,
within reason. You *would*, I mean, if you were hired.
You'll have to pardon my,
well,
suspicion but you're not what

usually applies for this job.

JESS. And "what" usually applies?

JOHN. Oh you know.

JESS. *(She does.)* No. Please tell me.

JOHN. I need someone who can really do this work so if you're
not willing to—
I'm sorry but—

JESS. A lot.

JOHN. What?

JESS. Of life.
Is how much I've lived.
So when a man tells me I'd hafta do some Various Things for him
for money, I gotta push that man for a little clarity.

JOHN. Okay.
Well when a woman says she went to Prince—

JESS. Cuz she did. She did. She says it, she writes it in her résumé,
cuz she did. She went to school, she's lived a lot of life—before and
after school—and she could do this. I could do this. If yer surprised
I'd be applyin for a job like this, while workin a buncha jobs like
those *(Re: résumé.)*, after goin to a place like this *(Re: school.)*, then
sorry, bro—

JOHN. John.

JESS. If a man like you—

JOHN. // Like what.

JESS. —livin how you do—

JOHN. And how's that?

JESS. If you don't understand why where I went to school, *that* I
went to school, doesn't mean shit for some people—then I dunno
what yer payin for in there.

JOHN. I'm fully funded // actually—

JESS. But I am not yer professor. Yer professor gets health insurance.

JOHN. Not necessarily—

JESS. I'd do whatever, okay?, whatever you needed.
I'd do whatever.

John.
Within reason.

Sorry—sorry I interrupted you.
>	*John looks at her.*
Please.
>	*John looks back down at the résumé.*
>	*It might look at first like defeat.*
>	*Perhaps Jess turns toward the door.*
>	*He looks back up.*

JOHN. Jess.

JESS. Yeah?

JOHN. -ica?

JESS. Just Jess.

JOHN. Early riser, *Jess?*

JESS. Can be.

JOHN. 6 A.M.?

JESS. *(Lying.)* …yup.

JOHN. Well then
>	*He extends his hand out to her.*
>	*A moment.*
>	*She watches it shake.*
>	*Then*
>	*she shakes his hand.*
Here we go.

Two.

Early September.
It's raining outside.

A different accessible apartment. In Jersey City, NJ. A largely
empty one, in transition and under-loved.

A woman enters. Ani.
She is in a wheelchair. Severe incomplete spinal cord injury.
Quadriplegic. Though some of the fingers of one hand are
partially functioning.
Ani is a woman whose world has not extended very far beyond
North Jersey and just you try to say something to her and
watch what happens. She has her own ways and she is fine
with those ways and those that do not agree don't need to
stick around—as many haven't. She can seem brusque or
intense to some people. A cat that resists being pet. Until it
wants to be.

Eddie enters with her, holding an umbrella over her. Then
remembers the umbrella.

EDDIE. Oh shit.
Bad luck.

> *Eddie closes the umbrella. Sets it aside.*
> *Their interactions used to have ease. Eddie muscles it now.*

So this is yer new...

> *He is surprised at the place. Takes it in.*

Ani.

You need to get some color in here. *(The worst.)* This beige?: No.
Feel like I'm walkin into a paper bag. You could get some kinda yellow in here. Some baby blue, some yellow. Good for emotions. I
read that. It's therapy. Colors work on yer feelings. Blue's for stress,
like—relief. Red's for passion.
And yellow I dunno but it's *yellow.*

Ask yer nurses. Watch. They'll tell you. Shit's science.

ANI. *(Bone dry.)* I thought I'd try yoga.
Fer my emotions.

EDDIE. ...Can you // do—?

ANI. NO.

EDDIE. Okay.

> *He looks around for something helpful to do.*

ANI. What're you doin // here—?

EDDIE. *(Looking for tasks.)* OkayOkayOkay. Pillow! Got yer pillow here.

> *He tries to put it somewhere behind her head or back. Sees she's strapped in all over...*

I'ma just fluff THAT.

> *...fluffs and sets the pillow aside.*

Okay. Blanket. Just blanket you with THAT.

> *He tucks a blanket around her chair.*

You lose weight?

> ...

I will punch myself later for that. On yer behalf.

Or—Y'know what:

> *He takes her paralyzed arm.*
> *She's confused at what's going on at first but has no control over it.*
> *Oh no. Is he really doing this?*
> *He is. He's really doing this. She can't believe he's doing this.*
> *He punches himself with her paralyzed hand.*
> *She doesn't look happy.*
> *He sees her face, not looking happy.*
> *And he awkwardly puts her hand back down by her side.*

ANI. The fuck is wrong // with you?

EDDIE. I don't know.

ANI. Strap it back in!

EDDIE. Sorry sorry.

He straps her wrist back on the arm of the chair.

ANI. Flatten it out.

EDDIE. What?

ANI. My fingers, you gotta—Flatten // out my—Or I'll lose those too.

EDDIE. Right.

He returns her hand to pre-fist position, flattening her fingers on the palm pad of her chair.

There you go.
You good?

ANI. Don't I look it?
What the fuck are you // doin here—?

EDDIE. The bed's the wrong way.

ANI. What?

EDDIE. Yer bed's faced away from the window.

ANI. Leave it.

EDDIE. Lemme move the bed.

ANI. Leave it.

EDDIE. Lemme just do this real // quick.

ANI. *(Finality.)* NO, EDDIE.
Just— // leave it.

EDDIE. Sorry. I do that.

ANI. Okay?

EDDIE. Okay.

ANI. Okay?

EDDIE. *Okay.*
damn.

ANI. But thank you.

EDDIE. *(Sass.)* You *would be* welcome.

ANI. Why were you just standin outside my place // in the rain like some—?

EDDIE. I'm just sayin you could get yerself some light. Ani. By the window. Light's good. Keeps you happy. Serotonin. Vitamins. There is vitamins in the sun that's only in the sun that—and we need it. So listen, it gets cloudy or rainy or some shit like this again 'n see if they'll get you a box.

One a those boxes with the light comin from it.

Get one 'n put it by yer face.

It's for serotonin.

It's supposed to shoot like, serotonin at yer face.

When there's none outside.

It's prob'ly covered in yer plan.

'N if not, you lemme know.

ANI. I'm still on yer plan.

EDDIE. Right.

ANI. So you'll know.

You'll know if I need a box.

To keep me happy.

EDDIE. True.

ANI. We can figure all that out, the insurance, soon's the papers—

EDDIE. We don't gotta // talk about that right now.

ANI. I'm just sayin that for now I'm on yer plan. 'Til the papers.

EDDIE. We can hold off on the papers. I'm sayin if you need. Fer the insurance.

They're just papers.

ANI. They're a lot more than that.

     …

Why are you here.

EDDIE. You look into that stuff I sent you?

ANI. What stuff?

EDDIE. I emailed you! Good stuff. Cuz those guys you go to?, they can move yer arms fer you, y'know, stretch you out or whatever they do on like the *physical* level, but there's other kinds of therapies you can do. They're prob'ly just givin you the basics over there.

ANI. So I should paint my fuckin walls is what yer sayin.

Then I'm cured.

EDDIE. Listen I have seen Miraculous Shit on YouTube. Actually, on the whole internet. It's good to have in yer back pocket, y'know, cuz insurance, my insurance, won't always…y'know.

ANI. You tryin to get rid of me?

EDDIE. What?

ANI. Off yer insurance? // Fast as you can? That's why yer here?

EDDIE. What?, no! I'm—no, man! All I'm sayin's maybe colors! Yellows. Blues. That's all I'm sayin. I dunno if you knew about em so I'm, now you know about em.
(Like he's not allowed to say it.) I…I've been thinkin about you.

ANI. When?

EDDIE. What?

ANI. Was it when I went unconscious from the sepsis? Was it then? When I woke up from the surgery. The second surgery. Or when they said I need one more. Maybe it was May. The day I learned to move a finger. Or was it just September. When I find you standin at my door. When exactly, Eddie, in the last six months since I saw you after the accident, did you think to think of me?

   …

EDDIE. I wasn't sure you wanted to see me.

ANI. What in the world would give you that idea.

   …

   …

EDDIE. There's also this thing I read says certain smells, right, // could—

ANI. I know.

EDDIE. You don't even know what I was gonna say.

ANI. That shit's not real.

EDDIE. What shit.

ANI. Colors. Smells. All that. Not real.

EDDIE. I dunno, I seen on YouTube—

ANI. Okay well my nurse is comin by at 7—

EDDIE. Oh cool good *cool.* So *she* // can tell you—

ANI. So you can go. You can go.

Thanks fer…settin me up.

I'm all set up now.

All set.

EDDIE. Yer welcome.

ANI. Bye.

EDDIE. Except…

ANI. What?

EDDIE. I texted you…about…

ANI. What?

EDDIE. There's just one // thing—

ANI. WHAT.

EDDIE. Except I gotta get my stuff?

I still gotta get some more of my stuff?

…

I texted? Last week. You, yer nurse, musta accidentally packed some of *my* stuff. I texted you about me comin by at some point to get my stuff. I called too. You ain't answer so—

ANI. So get yer stuff.

EDDIE. But I—okay—this is funny—so I kinda left forgot my, the, suitcases…at—

ANI. I don't have any suitcases.

EDDIE. So some are comin by.

ANI. Some…suitcases are comin by?

EDDIE. In a few.

ANI. Just…rollin by?

EDDIE. In a car.

ANI. She can't come in here.

…

EDDIE. You want me just to wait outside?

ANI. Yes I do.

EDDIE. *("Yer right.")* Okay.

…

…
In the rain?

ANI. Do what you want.

EDDIE. But like but what would you *prefer*?

ANI. Do what you want.

EDDIE. Okay.

ANI. Fuckin, *prefer*.

EDDIE. I'll wait right here then.

ANI. Then wait here.

EDDIE. Okay.

> *He waits.*

Want me to put on some music?

ANI. What is wrong with you?

EDDIE. No, not like—not like… *[sexy]* …*music*. Like…fer therapy.
// I read—

ANI. No.

EDDIE. Okay but yer not supposed to do like, homework or somethin,
some kinda physical therapy homework? After yer appointments?

ANI. You didn't read about it? On the whole internet?

EDDIE. How can I help? Ani. While I'm here, how can I help?

ANI. You don't gotta help me with shit. We're separated. Congratula-
tions on yer suitcases.

> …

EDDIE. I'll wait outside.

> *Ani watches—or senses—him walk toward the door.*

ANI. Sometimes they give you…physical therapy homework.

> *Eddie turns back.*

EDDIE. Like what?

ANI. *(Bone dry.)* Like "Try to move."
They do say I should listen to music.

EDDIE. See, I was tryin to tell you about that. And you'll do that?

ANI. It's not—

31

EDDIE. Do that. It works. I dunno how—they don't explain in the video— // but just *listen* to it—

ANI. I'm about to say some shit to you, Eddie, 'n I want you to hear it, okay?, so here's a Notice, an Advanced fuckin, that I'm about to say some shit I want you to hear. Okay?
You listening?

EDDIE. …yeah.

ANI. Don't interrupt me.

EDDIE. Yeah okay go.

ANI. I'm sad 'n I'm gonna—   EDDIE. You want the music?
        Let's try that again.

I'm sad 'n I'm gonna—I'M SAD.   You don't want the music?

ANI. *(Continued.)* 'N pissed. 'N I'm gonna be sad, pissed 'n sad, fer however long I'm pissed 'n sad, 'n that's fine. I feel like feelin whatever I feel right now. In my paper bag. 'N that's fine.

There's no recovery from this.
My spinal cord's shattered. This: Is it.
I know you know that so please just…don't. Okay?

I can mail you yer shit.
I mean not *me*. I can't, fuckin—But somehow I, yer shit will be mailed. The nurse can mail em.
I'll consider that box fer my face.

> *She sees Eddie on his phone.*

Are you // listening?

> *Suddenly, music.*
> *Eddie plays some music off his phone.*
> *Upbeat. And way too loud.*

EDDIE. How can you be sad with THIS?!?

> *He dances.*
> *He's having a GREAT time.*
> *He tries to involve her*
> *and then*
> *eventually*

he realizes how shitty that makes him
that he's dancing
and she can't.

And he stops.
The music still plays.

I can paint the walls // fer you.

ANI. Turn it off.

EDDIE. It's therapy, it can—

ANI. It's not. That's not therapy. Turn it off.

He turns it off.

…

You still can't dance.

…

…

…

EDDIE. Look who's talkin.

…

…

…

They look at each other.
And crack.
Laughter.
We can see why they were once good together.
There's a moment where they stop laughing.
And recognize that. And maybe this is both a good and bad thing.
Ani puts down her abrasion for a moment.

ANI. The way the therapist explained it

music

if you really wanna know

EDDIE. I'm listening.

She has had no one with which to share new information.

It's a vulnerable act. And he is listening.

ANI. …is when music plays, the body goes lookin for the things it's missing. The broken things. The shit that's disconnected. And it tries to bring everything back together. Like it used to be. Back in order. Order like…music.
(A dig, before he can contest her.) Classical shit.

The PT's helped me to *(She indicates she's moving her finger.)* a little, and just on that hand, but the music's supposed to…
You listen and…

    She moves the fingers of one hand as if playing piano.

yer body tries to imitate the…sense that music makes // which is why—

    Beep-beep.
    Car horn outside.

    There she is. The end of all that.

Can I just—can I just mail the stuff, Eddie?

EDDIE. That's expensive.

ANI. I'd rather mail it.

EDDIE. I'll just go get the bags // and—

ANI. I got an emergency button on this thing. I'll press the shit out of it I swear.

EDDIE. Who do you *[think I am?]*, cmon. You don't gotta threaten me // like I'm some kinda, fuckin—

ANI. I'm askin you then, then I'm askin you: Can I mail yer stuff. Say yes.

    He hovers by the door.

EDDIE. I'll send you the list. A list. Of my stuff.

ANI. Is she livin with you?
…In our…? In…Bayonne?

EDDIE. No.

ANI. Will she?

    …

EDDIE. *(Caught.)* …it's just cheaper fer us both to, instead of—

ANI. *("No more.")* Okay.

EDDIE. I can't pay fer a place on my own and help you at the same time.

ANI. I'll pay it back.

EDDIE. *(Not unkindly.)* Yeah but
but I'm payin it now.

    …

ANI. She's patient.

EDDIE. What?

ANI. Only beeped once.

EDDIE. I should head out.

ANI. Yeah.
Maybe you should.

EDDIE. Ani—

    He decides not to say whatever he was gonna say.

Don't worry about the stuff. Fuck the stuff, it's not important.

ANI. Which stuff?

EDDIE. It's nothin I can't live without.

    Eddie wonders if this is goodbye for a while.

Bye, Ani.

    He hovers by the door,
    sees if she'll look at him.
    She doesn't.
    And exits.
    Ani, alone.
    Silence.
    She takes in that she's alone.

    …
    …

    She closes her eyes.
    A finger moves.
    The fingers of one hand move.

As if playing piano. Or trying to.
She plays an invisible piano with a few of her fingers on one hand.

…

We watch her in silence.

…

Then, car engine.
A car drives away.
She opens her eyes.
No one.

Three.

September. Early morning.
John's apartment.
Jess' first day at work.

Jess prepares to shave John's face.

JESS. You tell me if I fuck up.
JOHN. If you
fuck up, you'll know.

> *Jess moves the razor to his face.*
> *About to do it but—*

Don't fuck up.

> *About to do it but—*

Tired?
JESS. There's a knife in my hand.

> *A breath, gets ready.*

Okay.

> *She shaves him.*
> *When the razor is far from his face—*

JOHN. Was it a long night?
At the bar?

> *She shaves him. Hesitantly.*

JESS. Yup.

JOHN. Me too. Long night.
Had a paper to write.
Tired?

JESS. *(Lying.)* Nope.

JOHN. I am.

JESS. It's not the same.

JOHN. What.

JESS. *(Re: shaving.)* It's hard to do this when yer talkin.

JOHN. I'm not
contagious.

JESS. What? I know.

JOHN. So come closer.

> *She does.*

"The better to see you with, my dear."

JESS. …What?

JOHN. Nothing.

> *She shaves him.*

I hired an English major who doesn't talk.

JESS. Who said I was an—

JOHN. Why else not list your
major? On your résumé.
Art history.

JESS. No.

JOHN. Ceramics.

JESS. No.

JOHN. Then tell me something
about yourself.

JESS. So you can make fun of me?

JOHN. No.
Depends.
Tell me something.

JESS. I can tell you I ain't cut you yet. I can tell you that.

JOHN. You're about to
see a lot of me. To know a lot of me.
You will take off my clothes and I will have nowhere to hide.
I don't really have a choice in that.

JESS. You had the choice to hire me.

JOHN. And my choices don't stop there.
Every morning you walk in here, I have a choice about that.

It would be nice to know
who is taking off my clothes.

JESS. You want a story?

JOHN. Or a vase. If that's how you
express.

JESS. I work at a bar. I drive there. In a car. Then I drive away.
I work at another bar. Take the train there, then I take the train back.
I work at bars. What do you want me to say? I went to college. This
one. And I work at a bar.
Bars.
The End.

JOHN. I'm just trying to talk.

JESS. Well I'm not my favorite thing to talk about.

JOHN. Why not—

JESS. You gonna tell me to smile fer you next?

JOHN. No—

JESS. Smile, sweetheart.

JOHN. // No—

She wipes his face with a towel.

JESS. I think yer good. No blood.

Jess moves away from John.
Perhaps John sits there a moment.
Alone. For just a moment.

38

JOHN. *(Kindly, one more try.)* Where are you from?

JESS. Okay what's next. Shower. Right. I shower you next.

> *No response.*
>
> *She takes it upon herself to try to manipulate his chair.*

Okay, let's go—

> *John moves himself away from her.*

JOHN. You want to just get it over with?

JESS. …What?

JOHN. You don't like to talk about yourself—Or to me—And you're
clearly—So let's just get this all out of the way.
The last thing I want to be reminded of every
morning, first thing in the—is how
uncomfortable my
body // makes—

JESS. I am not uncomfortable.

JOHN. Really?
Because I am.
The knees and elbows can't stop drawing

JESS. I am not uncomfortable with yer—I feel perfectly—Did I mess anything up?, Cuz I don't think I messed anything up. Try what.	JOHN. *(Continued.)* towards each other. I fight to keep them apart. The joints feel like magnets— Try it.

JOHN. What it would feel like.
Your knees and elbows—

JESS. Like pretend to be—Are you askin me to make fun of you?

JOHN. You are making fun of me
by thinking you'd be making fun of me.
It's part of the job.

JESS. The job's to shave you, shower you, brush yer teeth, to // get
yer—

JOHN. To take care of my body. Right. To understand me and
the needs of my body. That's your job.

JESS. And how's imitating you gonna help me shave yer face?

JOHN. I'm not asking you to—
Okay.
Okay.
Maybe this Maybe you
Maybe this just isn't working // out.

JESS. No, okay—Fuck—Look, I just started—

JOHN. If you treat me like a job—

JESS. You *are* my job.

JOHN. Like I'm not even—

JESS. You'd fire me cuz I don't wanna, what, mock you?

JOHN. No, // I'm not asking you to—

JESS. Cuz I didn't entertain you // on command?

JOHN. No, just—

JESS. I am not uncomfortable—

JOHN. *(The frustrated end of his rope.)* Then why can't we have a human conversation.
This was a mistake.

JESS. Most people assume my name's Jessica.
It's not.

My mother came to the country with no English, very little, and she's in this hospital in Newark—it's not there anymore this is clearly like a few years—and the nurse hands me to my mom for the first time. She was here alone. No family. And the nurse asks my mom like, what'll you call her? And my mom just looks at her. She said that's the moment it hit her, how alone she is. How little English. How everything now it's hers. Her shoulders. And she thought the nurse said—When my mom was asked a question, she'd usually either just say yes or no or okay like judgin on if it was a man or a woman she was answerin, or if they looked nice, I mean most times people just asked her like, do you want a bag or are you okay and so she says yes or no or I'm okay. And so my mom, when the nurse asked my name, she I think she meant to say yes but, in her, y'know, her accent...

So my name's Jess.

Just Jess.
They were nice enough to put two S's.

     …

JOHN. You tell everyone that story? That's your
story, right?, that you tell everyone?

JESS. Y'know what how 'bout I just finish the job and you can
judge me on that. So shower. // I'll shower you now.

JOHN. I didn't mean to judge you—

> *Jess reaches carelessly for John's shirt, as if to undress him.*
> *The surprising, forceful contact causes John to spasm and splay.*
> *Jess pulls away, instinct.*
> *John risks falling out of the chair but catches himself.*
> *Jess freezes, doesn't know what to do.*
>
> *Throughout the following, John recovers.*
> *At some point Jess assists him in a small way.*

My body—
if you get too close, too fast—

My body over-protects itself.

Any time I reach beyond myself,
it's violence.
You reach and you shake and
it always feels beyond you.
So you have to throw yourself—your
arms, your hands—at what you want.

> *He grabs her arm.*
> *Holds her.*

Have you ever been hit?

     …

Have you ever been—

JESS. Why.

JOHN. That's what it's like. Under my skin. From underneath
my skin. Like people hitting me
from beneath my skin.

> *He lets her go.*

41

And that's what you'll be working with. Every morning. Is touching, shaving,
undressing,
washing
and clothing—that.
That's what I'm like.

>*They stand apart a moment.*

JESS. That the story *you* tell everyone?

JOHN. No, actually.
No one ever asks.

JESS. Well I clearly wasn't gonna.

JOHN. And I don't like to talk about it.

JESS. Why did you?

JOHN. Because I never did.

You're the
first, my
first
I ever hired on my own.
Since I started living on my own.

I never…

>*Something feels unsatisfactory to John.*
>*He goes back to logistics.*

There's an aftershave lotion
you can use.

JESS. What else you never done?

JOHN. What?

JESS. You said you never…so…
What else, John, have you never done?

>*Something new is beginning.*

Tell me something
about yourself.

Four.

October.
Evening. Ani's apartment.

ANI. Hell no.

EDDIE. But I know you, yer body—

ANI. More reason fer No. You knew how fuckin amazing it *was*.

EDDIE. I need the money.

ANI. Why? Fer her?

EDDIE. No. Fer like, in general.
Cmon, you'd rather have a stranger, some kinda—stranger comin in to take care of you? You don't know people, Ani.

ANI. I knew *you* 'n see what happened?

EDDIE. Y'know it's really hard to talk to you when all you got is trumps on me.

ANI. I'm not hiring you.

EDDIE. Discrimination.

ANI. Fine. Cuff me.

EDDIE. You wouldn't hafta pay me as much as someone else.

ANI. How's what's-her-fuck feel about this?

EDDIE. Great.

ANI. She has no idea.

EDDIE. No, we definitely communicated about it. You really got a button?

ANI. What? // Yes I do.

EDDIE. An emergency button, you got one? Then press it.

ANI. No.

EDDIE. Press it.

ANI. No.

EDDIE. Press it.

ANI. No!

43

EDDIE. Press it if you don't want me here.
Press it.

ANI. I really gotta say, Eddie, that I never got as huge an urge to get the fuck outta this chair as when I saw yer fuckin face. Since I seen you last month? The weaponry that's been dancin in my dreams, the violence that I would like to do to you is so—creative that that's when I feel like I could just vault outta my body. Outta this chair. Those moments are my most alive.

EDDIE. So hire me.

   …

You been thinkin about me?

ANI. What?

EDDIE. Since "last month."

   Perhaps he sings/dances a bit, as in their first scene.

ANI. Get the fuck outta my house.

EDDIE. Ani, whatever I don't understand now about…, I will. I learn fast.
Just gimme a week. Just gimme a trial run fer like, a week.

ANI. Yer here cuz you feel like a fuck.

EDDIE. I always felt like a fuck. I'm just variations of that feeling from day to day.

ANI. And when you quit feelin like the lowest of a fuck, however or whoever makes you feel even half a rung higher, then you'll leave. I know you.

EDDIE. You know that One Time that happened.

ANI. Yer *livin* with her in our place in Bayonne, that's more than once.

EDDIE. We were separating. At the time, the first time, you 'n I were—We're // separated!

ANI. Right. I know you.

EDDIE. That's right. That's right you do know me. You know me as a man who's been twelve years sober. A man who's been twenty—almost one—years faithful. I wasn't some perfect // fuckin y'know, but—

ANI. Yup.

EDDIE. But I was pretty good, Ani. You can't deny the numbers. Twelve. Twenty-almost-one.

Not spotless, especially with the—But pretty good. Shit, compared to—

ANI. What.

Me?

EDDIE. To before.

Compared to *me* before. Twelve years ago 'n then the nine before that? Compared to that, I done pretty good. That part I don't need you to confirm fer me. I know that. I know I got far. I know that in like, myself. That I come a long way. With that shit?, with me before?, a *week* is far.

(A quiet truth.) Proud of that. So.

I've taken care of you before. When you were goin through // yer own—

ANI. *(Not proud of this, "stop talking.")* Okay.

EDDIE. Not tryin to hold that over you. I know what that is, to hafta be taken care of. I'm just sayin…you seen my work.

ANI. Yer what?

EDDIE. You woke up the next day. You ain't die. So I guess that's my like, work sample. Yer my work sample.

ANI. I was blacked out fer most of yer work sample.

EDDIE. Like I said, you ain't die.

Look, how much money you actually have to spend? How much would this cost you to get someone—?

ANI. I get checks. And I've applied for // some things.

EDDIE. And all the hidden costs? I got a nice fat report from The Internet about THAT.

ANI. I'd rather find some way to pay someone than just hang on yer insurance forever like a fuckin, or on to you—

EDDIE. How? // How would you—?

ANI. I dunno, man, but I'd rather do that!

EDDIE. And go a few days without bathing? Having brushed teeth? Eating?

ANI. I'd rather find someone I can trust—

EDDIE. Like yer nurse tonight?

ANI. This is one time This is one time this is happened She had her schedule wrong probably she probably had her schedule wrong.

EDDIE. Just this one time, she fucked up. This the only time?

ANI. Just this time.

EDDIE. And yer okay with that? Yer okay with that? You'd trust her again? To show up? To do what she's gotta do?

ANI. …

EDDIE. Just once.
Like me.

ANI. What do you think's gonna happen you come take care of me a few hours a day? Huh? You brush my teeth a couple mornings, dump my bedpan a few times and BOOM, consc*[ience]*—fuck-shit, clap yer hands when I say Boom.

EDDIE. What?	ANI. You dump my bedpan and BOOM—clap yer hands.

EDDIE. Like, // applause—?

ANI. CLAP. Like one clap.
And BOOM, clap yer—CLAP YER—

> *He claps.*

Not yet! Aaaand BOOM—

> *He claps.*

Aaaand BOOM.

> *He claps on BOOM.*

And BOOM—

> *He claps on BOOM.*

And BOOM—

> *He claps on BOOM.*

And BOOM

> *He claps.*

and BOOM

> *He claps.*

and BOOM

He claps.

—You dump my bedpan a few times and BOOM

He claps.

—conscience cleared?

...

EDDIE. ...This what you did with yer nurse? Maybe this is why she ditched you.

ANI. Yer not doin penance on me.

EDDIE. Yer right cuz yer not my fault. This wasn't my fault.
You right now?, The way you are?:

He claps.

Not my fault.
Look I know you won't forgive me fer the—I know that. Even though we were separated.
Technically. Which, I mean maybe you'll forgive // me but—Okay.

ANI. Nope.

EDDIE. All I can hope for then, I guess, is some kinda shift. Not forgiveness I guess but. I dunno.
I can just hope fer something like that.
But I didn't do this to you. So.
So, no, I don't owe you penance for that.

I'd be doin a service. Fer free. Or at a real cheap rate, if you need that to make it feel...whatever.
And temporary.

ANI. ...

EDDIE. ...

ANI. You know what we talk about? My nurse 'n me? What we talked about? Nothin usually. She'd ask me how I'm doin, how this 'n that feels. Any problems? Physical problems? The weather.
Straightforward shit like that. She tells me the weather all over America. We sympathize over snow in Chicago. We shake our heads at the humidity in Atlanta. We sigh about Minnesota. That must be awful, we say. That must be so awful fer people. Wherever she's got family, I know about it. I know about what their days must

47

be cuz she tells me their weather.

I fuckin love that bitch.

EDDIE. …it's still raining outside but it's supposed to // clear up tomorrow.

ANI. And it's nice—It is sometimes real nice to just think about someone's weather. To feel bad fer their snow.

To forget I used to live a different way.

To forget what other people gotta do for me that I can't anymore.

That I did this to myself.

EDDIE. You didn't—

It was an acci*[dent]* —Bad luck.

I'm sorry.

I'll never bring that up again.

ANI. We got too many trumps on each other. Decades of em.

I can see why you'da gone to her. It's nice to talk about other things…the weather…sometimes.

…

Okay, I'm done. No more of that talk.

New apartment. New body. New life. Old nurse.

EDDIE. Could I just try?

ANI. Why?

EDDIE. Cuz you don't have much of a choice in it.

ANI. …Why don't I?

EDDIE. Cuz I already told em I'd take care of things.

ANI. I do have a button.

EDDIE. Okay. And it went right to me.

I'm yer emergency contact.

I'm still yer emergency contact.

So when it turned out yer nurse couldn't come tonight, they called me.

I said I'd go over 'n check on you.

I said I would

'n I'm here.

ANI. …I can change those forms.

EDDIE. 'N who would you put? Who do we know in our lives who'd come? Who's got the money or the... *[responsibility]* ...who you think could do this?

...

Can I—please—try to help you this week?
I've got a week before I hafta head out again for a drive. Seven days.
Seven.
Just the nights.
Seven nights, starting tonight.
ANI. Why?
EDDIE. If I fuck up, I'm gone. They're findin you someone new anyways but fer now—
ANI. But—why, Eddie?
EDDIE. Cuz I'd like to see you.

...

Seven nights.

...

Ania?*

...

Something shifts for Ani.
She sees her lot.

...

ANI. My birthday.

It's my birthday next month. Three weeks.

I forgot.

...

...

I'll be 42.

...

EDDIE. *(As though he is the present.)* Happy Birthday, Baby.

* Pronounced [anya]. See note on casting.

Five.

December.
John's apartment.

Jess showers John.
We watch the entire act.
It takes as long as it needs.

Jess wheels John into the shower.
She helps lift him from his wheelchair onto his shower seat.
How this happens: John embraces Jess, who he uses as support.
Jess holds on to John as he pushes himself up and pivots on his
toes from the wheelchair to the shower seat.
She undresses him completely.
She runs the water.
Tests it on herself.
Tests it on his arm.
He nods if it's okay.
She washes his hair.
She soaps his body and rinses it off.

Jess picks up a conversation she began earlier.
There is more ease between the two now.

JESS. I mean I don't love these women either—sometimes they're worse than the but I'm not givin the girl tequila when she's that fuckin *done*, y'know.

JOHN. Naturally.

JESS. Especially when she ain't order it. I mean I'll take a man's money whatever but No Rapes On My Watch. This girl's on the couches we got, in the back, right, half dressed, half asleep (and this place is not, y'know, it's *loud*), and this guy to me he's like, YO cmere. Like 'Ey-oh!, OVER HERE. And he's one of those, y'know, with the button dooooown—

JOHN. Right.

JESS. jeeeeans

JOHN. *(Judgment.)* God.

JESS. with the hair, y'know what I'm sayin?

JOHN. Oh yes.

JESS. And orange. He tans. Bro, it's fuckin December. And he's like This girl needs a *shot.* So I'm like Listen Chief I think she's *good.* And he's like Listen bitch—

JOHN. Uh-oh.

JESS. Who's got the money, he says, and who the fuck are you?

JOHN. Wow.

JESS. And he throws this balled-up dollar in my face.

JOHN. Some people.

JESS. Bouncer palmed his greasy head 'n threw his douche ass out.

JOHN. Good.

JESS. Right in the snow. Man, fuck rich people. No offense but, heads on sticks. France should happen here.

    A moment of silent showering.

I don't understand why people here gotta judge you by yer job. I'm not my job.

JOHN. People have to judge you by something.

JESS. Except no the fucks don't.

JOHN. How else will they know if they're
winning or not?

JESS. I don't judge people.

    John makes a judgmental noise.

I make a sincere effort not to judge people.

JOHN. Well I hope you never drown.

JESS. I hope you never drown too, John.

JOHN. Because if it's you and Michael
Phelps and I
swimming in the Hamptons and you get a cramp? And you call
on
me because you're not judgmental?
I think you'd probably die.

51

...

I judged you.

JESS. How'd you judge me?
Here, you want yer— *(Wash cloth.)*

JOHN. Yes please, here—

JESS. Got it?

JOHN. Got it, thanks.

> *Jess puts into John's hand a soaped up wash cloth.*
> *He uses this to wash his genitals.*
> *Jess turns away so he can have privacy.*
> *It's not awkward. Routine.*

JESS. How'd you judge me?

JOHN. Well.
I think.
I judged you well,
I think.
You haven't
lost me.

> *He drops the cloth on the shower floor—he's done with it. She*
> *rinses him.*

JESS. You don't gimme the chance to lose you.
You barely leave.

JOHN. I leave.

JESS. To class, maybe.

JOHN. I don't *just* go to class.

JESS. I never see you go out.

JOHN. Big campus.

JESS. The neighborhood, even. This area. When I leave, after I'm
done here every morning, you usually just—hang.

JOHN. I don't like to be rushed.

JESS. Never see you, all I'm sayin.

JOHN. Well
I never see you.

JESS. When would you be seein me? I don't live here.
I don't even come around here except fer you.

JOHN. I—
I never see you,
except when you're working,
is all I'm saying.

JESS. I don't go out much.

JOHN. At all.

JESS. It's cold.

JOHN. Not all the—

JESS. Lately, yeah! Lately it's been cold as—And, man, anyways, you go out, you spend money. Coffee. Fuckin, ham sandwich. All that's money.

JOHN. So you, what,
stay home? Read? The cereal
box I guess because books are "money."

          ...

JESS. I work.

JOHN. Okay but
You can't It's not
possible to work all the—

JESS. You can. People can. They do.

JOHN. That doesn't seem like
a life.

          The silence of task-doing.

JESS. I sleep.
For fun.

          She has lain a towel on the wheelchair.
          She lifts him from his shower seat and helps situate him onto
          his wheelchair.
          Dries his body.

JOHN. Why—For what are you
working so much?

          ...

53

JESS. Everything.

> *She puts on his pants. Shoes.*

(To herself.) Who's got the money, he says, and who the fuck are you.

JOHN. Don't worry about that—

JESS. He's right though.

JOHN. No he's a—

JESS. It does matter who you are.
And what you have.
It matters.

> ...

JOHN. Well
I think as long as you—

JESS. —work hard?

> *She works.*

Those guys I serve at the bar? They make more in an hour—with a finger—than I make in a week with my whole entire body.

It matters who you are. Family. Connections. If there's gonna be a net when you fall.
Cuz everybody falls.

I'm the first one born in this country. And I'm the only one left—
I was supposed to be the one to—

I was supposed to be the net.

JOHN. Is there something going on?

JESS. I'm just exhausted.

JOHN. What's going on?

> *She looks at him.*
>
> *She considers for a moment whether to tell him what's going on. Decides against it.*

JESS. Polo or V-neck?

JOHN. Crew, please.
The olive one.

> *Jess retrieves a shirt.*

JESS. Nice. Is this another new one?

JOHN. I may have even *gone out* for it.

She dresses him.

JESS. So how'd you judge // me?

JOHN. What about merit?

JESS. …What about it?

JOHN. Aside from family and—
Doesn't merit count for something?

JESS. Depends.
On who's the judge.

JOHN. Well you're not
not-privileged either.

Jess was about to contradict him.
Then realizes what he's referring to.

JESS. No.
No, I'm not not-privileged either.

JOHN. And you're not
completely alone.

Jess doesn't reply.

You've got me in any case.

JESS. My employer.

JOHN. Your…well…

JESS. What? You pay me.

JOHN. Yes but.

But

I'm here.

…

(Re: attractiveness.) And also you're…
I mean in terms of
"things you've got going for you."
You're also…

JESS. What.

JOHN. Cmon.

JESS. What.

JOHN. You know.

JESS. No, what.

...

JOHN. Can you um
can you fix my—

JESS. Yeah.

She adjusts his clothes. She is close to him.

JOHN. You um...

JESS. Yeah?

JOHN. You smell good.

Jess and John feel how close they are to each other.

JESS. Perfume.
Samples.

I take em from magazines.

JOHN. It's nice.

JESS. It's prob'ly yer soap. On me.

Jess moves away to return to work.

So how did you judge // me—?

JOHN. Your body.

This catches Jess.

For one.

Was that a compliment? Flirtation?

Whether you can
lift me.

...

JESS. Okay.
And?

JOHN. And how you
move.

JESS. And how's that?

JOHN. Why don't you go out?

JESS. Much

JOHN. At all. Why
not? Someone like you?

...

JESS. *(A dare; she knows what he means.)* Someone like what, John.

JOHN. *(Knows she knows what he means.)* And because you went
to school here. Was another way I judged you.
It means you're not a dumbass.

JESS. Yer not gonna say it?

JOHN. Fuck nope, Jess.
Quite right.
Fuck nope.

> *Jess should have finished dressing John by now. She takes in
> her work.*

How do I look?

JESS. Good.

JOHN. Good.

...

Good.

JESS. *(Preparing to leave, putting on a winter coat.)* Okay, well if—

JOHN. Are you around tonight?

JESS. Am I, around?

JOHN. This—...?

JESS. Friday night?

JOHN. Would you
want to come over?

JESS. "Come over"?

JOHN. At 7?

JESS. You don't usually ask me to come by at night.

JOHN. I know.

JESS. And on a Friday night.

JOHN. I know it's late // notice—

JESS. *(Finality.)* Yes. Yeah. I would. I wanna come over. Tonight.

     ...

JOHN. Yeah?   JESS. Wait.

JESS. Lemme um, lemme just call 'n see if I can—

JOHN. Right.
No of course. // Right.

JESS. No y'know what Fuck it.

JOHN. No, don't // do that.

JESS. Someone'll cover. I'm sure. Fuck it. Yes.

     She's convincing no one.

JOHN. Are you // sure?

JESS. *(Rapid-fire.)* It's just—Friday night, I make the most on—and they're hard to, y'know, cuz you gotta work *up* to—They start you on Mondays Tuesdays shit days 'til you—Fridays are—And they don't always give em back if—Which is fucked—And there won't be as much—cuz, December now—And Fridays are—no yeah— yeah no—But everyone wants—But no yeah no someone'll want that. Someone'll take that. Someone'll jump on a Friday shift.
I'll see you at seven.

JOHN. ...Are you // sure?

JESS. Yes.

JOHN. Yeah?

     ...

JESS. Yeah.
Love to.
I'd love to come over. Tonight.

Yes.

JOHN. Good.

JESS. Good.

JOHN. Cool.

     She wipes some saliva that has collected on his mouth,
     perhaps with a little extra care and sensuality.

JESS. Cool.

JOHN. Tonight.

JESS. Yeah okay.

> *She looks at him. A spark in her.*

Tonight.

> *And she exits the bathroom.*
> *With some sass in her step.*

Six.

> *October. Ani's apartment.*
> *Ani is being sponged in a bath by Eddie.*
>
> *A radio on.*
> *It plays quietly in the background.*
>
> *We watch them a while.*

ANI. I fuckin hate this.

EDDIE. I know you do.

ANI. Cuz it woulda been good to feel this before. To have had you do this kinda stuff with me before.

It's nice.

You fuckin prick.

> *A moment of washing.*

You coulda done this when it // mattered—

EDDIE. How's the water?

ANI. Good.
I'm tired of yellin at you.

EDDIE. Me too. Of you yellin at me.

ANI. I've thrown every awful string a words I could think of at you these past few days 'n I'm a very creative // person but yer still here.

EDDIE. That's true you had some good lines.

ANI. You come back.
I thought you'da gone but yer here.
I don't trust that. There's something about that I don't trust.
EDDIE. Say the word 'n I'll go.

    …

ANI. Yeah I don't trust that. You'll be back.

    A moment of washing.

How's the water feel?
EDDIE. Hm?
ANI. To you?, how's it feel?
EDDIE. Oh shit is it too cold? Shit sorry. // Sorry sorry.
ANI. No no no. It's good for me.
I'm askin fer you. How's it feel to you?
Yer hands are in it too.
I just don't want it to be too cold fer you either.
Also.
I also want it to be nice fer you.

You prick.
EDDIE. That's nice of you.
ANI. It is, prick. I know.
EDDIE. *(Re: the water.)* It's great.
Thank you.
It's great fer me.

    His hands reach into the tub.
    Between her legs.

    They stay there a minute. Frozen.
    Or pull away.

    …

ANI. You *can.*
EDDIE. What?

    A look.

Oh.
Oh.

ANI. You may have um
noticed
when you were—

EDDIE. // uh huh

ANI. undressing me // that—

EDDIE. Yeah.

> *She pauses for Eddie to get it.*
> *Eddie is getting something completely different.*

I don't think I should, Ani. It might complicate // things—

ANI. No so I started bleeding, it's my // —this morning—

EDDIE. Oh!
Right.

ANI. See this is why I wanted a lady to do this.

EDDIE. No no I can, it's not // weird. I can—

ANI. I'm not askin you to...inside, I'm—jesus—It's not any sorta
wild—action that I'd need ya to do here. I just I know you usually
avoid that area. In general. Lately. *(Sudden embarrassment.)* jesus
christ.

EDDIE. It's fine.

ANI. Just since yer cleaning, // y'know, *around* that area—

EDDIE. It's okay.
It's fine it's fine.

…

It's fine.

Like this?

> …
> …

ANI. Yeah.
EDDIE. It's fine.

> …

ANI. I can't feel much.
Of anything. There.

61

I just want you to know in case yer like...feelin weird.
EDDIE. I'm not.
I don't feel weird.
Totally normal.
ANI. I'm not sayin I don't. Or I won't. I could.

I feel that...kind of feeling.

It's just not on that part of my body.

> ...

EDDIE. Where is it?

> ...

ANI. It's somewhere else.

> ...

> *The sound of hands in water.*

> ...

I imagine things.
It's all imagining now. I imagine things.
EDDIE. What things?
ANI. Nice things.

In case you were wondering.

That's what I do these days.
My mind is a great lover.

> *Ani rethinks.*

It's a good lover.

It's my memory I worry about. My mind's limited. I can only really imagine...variations of what already happened in my life. But in like, slightly different ways. So my imagination's got all this...grime that won't come off it from my memories.

> *Eddie's hands in the water*
> *are doing something to Ani*
> *that she has loved for years.*
> *We should not know this has been happening until we hear*
> *how he talks to her—*

EDDIE. You can't feel this?

What I'm doin right now?

        …

You can't feel that?

        …

        …

        …

ANI. No.

> *Eddie stops.*
> *And he continues washing.*
> *A song of slow piano from the radio. Perhaps Satie.*

EDDIE. You listenin to this song?

ANI. Hm?, what?
Yeah.
Yeah it's nice don't change it.

EDDIE. You wanna learn to play it?

ANI. Hilarious.

EDDIE. No I mean I can't play it either. Not like, traditionally.
Always wanted to learn though. Anything. Any kinda instrument.
The sax. // Or, y'know, or maybe the piano.

ANI. God, not the fuckin *sax*. Oh yeah piano, okay.

EDDIE. Think it woulda been cool to learn.

ANI. Well.
You still could.

EDDIE. Used to pretend I could. My folks, they got me this little
keyboard for Christmas once. Li'l Casio. They thought I'd be a
champ at it. Long fingers, y'know. And I wanted to learn, Tried but.
Nothing. And it killed me cuz I mean they *bought* it—with money
they ain't really have, y'know. They bought it without realizin how
much lessons cost and that school don't give em.
So I'd pretend to be able to play.
There was this control on it where you could still play it but no
sound had to come out. So I'd imagine what it'd sound like. To play.
If I could.

I'd put the radio on. Find the station where they play piano. And I'd act like I was playin that. Beautiful stuff. I'd act like that was me playin that.

...

(Re: radio.) It's a good song.

ANI. You never told me.

EDDIE. Hm?

ANI. You never told me that.

> *They listen.*
>
> *Then,*
> *Eddie takes one of Ani's arms,*
> *and drapes it along the bathtub edge.*

What're you doin?

> *Eddie rests one hand on her arm,*
> *then the other*
> *and he begins to "play" Ani's arms like a piano.*
> *He mimes the music that's playing on the radio.*
> *It should look like the music is coming from Ani's body.*

> *He's good.*
> *He knows the song.*
> *His fingers are beautifully accurate with the piano music.*

> *It lasts long enough to move something in the two.*

EDDIE. Always wish I could.

> *He plays.*

You feel that?

...

...

...

ANI. Yeah.

...

He stops playing.

...

EDDIE. What do you wanna do fer yer birthday?
Weather's supposed to be nice next month.

ANI. It'll be November. In New Jersey.
And you can't tell weather that far in advance.

EDDIE. We can plan on it bein nice. 'N if it's not, then we'll roll
with it.

ANI. "We"?

EDDIE. What would you wanna do?

ANI. You won't be here.

EDDIE. Why not?

ANI. You got yer drive.

EDDIE. What if I took off?

ANI. 'N what if you paid yer bills?
Don't take off work.

EDDIE. Listen woman I'm gonna do what I'm gonna do.

ANI. *(Not unkindly.)* Don't promise me things, Eddie.

...

EDDIE. What would you wanna do?
          Ani looks at him suspiciously.

ANI. Mm. You wouldn't like it.

EDDIE. It's not about me.

ANI. Maine.
I wanna go to Maine.
Fer my birthday.

    …
    …

EDDIE. It's cold up there // right?

ANI. See?

EDDIE. And it rains a lot and it's all like, fancy boats 'n shit? // Lobsters.

ANI. Yer thinkin of Seattle.

EDDIE. They got fancy boats there too, right?

ANI. Maybe. Never been. That's why I wanna go.

EDDIE. Okay yeah but Maine? That's like—Canada. Why you wanna go to Maine?

ANI. I saw this picture once on Janey's desk—some trip she took with her kids after the divorce. To Maine. // The—

EDDIE. Like, a photo? You wanna go to Canada cuz of a—?, shit, I'll show you some photos of Cancún, you'll change yer mind about, fuckin, Canada.

ANI. The frame was made outta wood but like, real wood. It was just four little twigs tied together but somehow it looked nicer than if someone tried to fix it into wood. And Janey's got a hat on—cuz it's so *sunny* in Maine—so you can't see her eyes but you can see her mouth which looked…
It's her in a field and she's holdin a stick like a cane. It's just her…by herself…and she's…fine.
And there's a lot of green.

EDDIE. Is that…? Is that where you were goin? That night?

ANI. That's what they told me later. When the ambulance found me, they said that's what I said.
I wasn't. But.
But maybe I would've. If I'd kept drivin.

66

I'd hafta change a bunch of doctor's appointments if I went anywhere fer my birthday.

EDDIE. Yeah but. Yer birthday!

ANI. Yeah but I don't wanna fuck around. With appointments. And it costs a lot to…do anything. Fer me to do anything.

Don't take off work.

EDDIE. I tore up the papers.

ANI. What?

EDDIE. Or I will.
I will. When I get home.
The divorce papers.

ANI. Don't talk about papers right now.

EDDIE. Okay.

ANI. Papers were trees.

> *A moment of not talking.*

EDDIE. Can you smoke in here?

ANI. I can do anything I want in here.

> *Eddie lights a cigarette.*
> *He alternates puffs between them, using his hands.*
> *One for him. One for her. For him. For her.*
> *They don't need language for this.*
> *He knows she'd want some.*
>
> *The following is quiet and simple.*
> *They know each other better than anyone.*

She leave you?

EDDIE. What?

ANI. Did she leave you?

EDDIE. No.

Not yet.

But the…clouds are there.

ANI. People are hard.

> *They smoke.*

What are you gonna do?

...

...

EDDIE. Is there a world, Ani, where...where you and—?
ANI. No.

...

...

We should think he understands. And drops it.
But—
EDDIE. Why not?
ANI. *(Not antagonistically, just clear-eyed.)* If I give you reasons,
Eddie, you'll just—talk. It's not a game where you gather up all yer
points fer this 'n pit em against all my points fer that 'n who's right 'n
who's wrong. It's not like that anymore. If you wanna help me, you
can help me. You helped me. But if you ever came back,...like, Came
Back...I'd need to know it was fer me. Not fer...anything else.

(A rare glimpse into her longing.) If I weren't like this right now,
would you be here?

...

EDDIE. Yeah.
Yes.

...

ANI. That's not a thing I'll ever know.
Everything's started over fer me—
EDDIE. It doesn't have to though.
ANI. If everything was perfect in yer life, no holes you had to fill,
you wouldn't be here.
EDDIE. That's not how people work. People don't go after people
unless they fuckin need em. And everyone fuckin—needs em,
someone. That's what life is, what yer life, my life...is. Okay?
That's how people work. In life.

Where's yer ashtray?
ANI. They prob'ly didn't pack it. Fer fuckin, my own fuckin good

'n shit, the fucks.
Check the kitchen though.

EDDIE. Be back. Don't go anywhere.

> *Eddie gets up to exit the bathroom.*

ANI. Hey.

> *He stops.*

EDDIE. What's up?

ANI. It's been nice to get to know you.
Again.
This week.

EDDIE. You too.

ANI. You prick.

EDDIE. Maybe you'll take me to Maine one day.

ANI. Yeah.
Maybe.
Maybe I'll see you there one day.

EDDIE. Or you'll take me. I wiped yer fuckin ass this week—

ANI. Oh my // God.

EDDIE. Fer *free*. You owe me fuckin—Canada.

ANI. Go to the fuckin kitchen.

> *He smiles at her.*
> *She smiles at him.*
> *The pricks.*

EDDIE. Be back.

> *Eddie leaves the room.*
>
> *Ani alone.*
> *She sits with herself in the tub.*

ANI. *(To offstage Eddie.)* I think I'm gonna go back to work. In a few months. See Janey. Everyone. What do you think? Think I'll do that. I'd like to.

> *She awaits a response.*

Eddie?

> *He can't hear her.*

She stares out. Sits with herself in the tub.
She starts to wonder where he is.
Tries to turn her head.

Eddie? Did you hear—

Suddenly, she slips down into the tub.
Not intentional.
Becomes submerged.

We hear yelling from underwater.

From off, we hear rummaging in the kitchen.

Eventually, Eddie returns, holding a plate for an ashtray.
He drops the plate and reaches into the tub
to retrieve Ani. She gasps for air.

He holds her against him.

She gasps.

You can't leave me in the—
You can't leave me in—

EDDIE. I'm sorry.

ANI. You can't—
You can't—
You—

EDDIE. I'm sorry.

She gasps.

ANI. Don't go.

He holds her to him.

Seven.

Friday evening.
John's apartment.

Nice lighting.
Music plays.

Jess enters. She carries a black plastic shopping bag. Sets it down.
She shakes snow off of her. Takes off her coat.
She's dressed up. DTF. Lookin good. Feelin good.
She takes in the music and mood-lighting. Impressive.

She adjusts her dress. Tights. Hair.
Pulls a magazine sample of perfume from her bag
and applies it to her chest and maybe under her arms.
She looks back to see if he might be coming
and then she also applies some between her thighs.

She poses, ready.

JESS. John?

> *Flush, offstage.*

JOHN. *(Off.)* You're
early.

> *John enters.*
> *He turns off the music with a remote.*

You're dressed so—

JESS. Yeah.

JOHN. Nice.

JESS. It's true.

JOHN. You look nice.

JESS. Well, you only see me in the mornings so—

JOHN. I need a shower, though, and // you're all—

JESS. Oh. A—?

71

(Intrigued.) Yeah?
Yeah okay.

JOHN. Could we maybe
start with a shower?

JESS. I can get into that.

JOHN. I know this is a bit
different
from our usual—

JESS. Uh-huh.

JOHN. And then maybe a shave.
An extra good shave.

JESS. I can do that.

JOHN. I thought if it was too early, like
early in the week or this morning, if you shaved me too early,
I'd be prickly.

JESS. Cuz yer a fuckin gentleman like that.

JOHN. And you're
good at it.
And…

JESS. Uh-huh…

JOHN. And I'm nervous.

JESS. You don't hafta be nervous.

JOHN. And excited!

JESS. Well it's good to talk before.

JOHN. I used to consider hookers.

JESS. Yeah but maybe let's not talk about that.

JOHN. Yes that's not a very manly conversation. I used to think
when I spoke of
hookers it would be manly.

JESS. Don't talk about hookers.

JOHN. But I just wouldn't know where to start
looking for—see, another unmanly, I simply shouldn't ever talk
about hookers.

JESS. No.

JOHN. But if we don't talk about how far we've come, Jess, not doing certain things, how will anyone know how far we've come?

JESS. What do you wanna do first?

JOHN. Brag.

JESS. Well how bout I could shave you first.

JOHN. Good plan.

JESS. Then shower.

JOHN. Yes.

JESS. So the cream, the—

JOHN. Right. I see where you're going with that.

JESS. —the shaving cream would get washed right off yer body. In the shower.

JOHN. Do we have time for both?

JESS. Fuck yes.

JOHN. I'm meeting her at 8.

     …

JESS. Wait.

JOHN. *(In his own world.)* Mm. What time is Maybe I should skip one. If I had to skip one, shower or shave: which?

JESS. For a…

JOHN. First date!

JESS. With a…
Hooker? JOHN. Graduate student!

JOHN. Madelyn.
From *Oxford*.
From *actual* Oxford.
PhD with a focus in *Hume*,
the minx.
I'm meeting her at 8. Just like her figure.
How does one even do this. When someone's so *[wonderful]*—
There's just something so *[wonderful]* about her.

73

Amidst this, while John is oblivious,
Jess takes from her plastic bag a bottle of wine.
Opens it. A twist-off. Pours a glass.

What is this?

JESS. Pinot.

She puts a straw in his glass.

JOHN. Good idea.

He drinks from the straw. And wonders.

Oh Jess.
Jess Jess.
How does one do it?

She drinks from the bottle.

JESS. *(As if to herself.)* Shave and a shower.

JOHN. Shave and a shower, yes.
Please.
Thank you.

JESS. What time you gonna be done?

JOHN. What?

JESS. With yer date.

JOHN. Well that
depends. *Late*, I hope.
Oh, but you don't have to wait up.
You can go after this. And I can
pay you for the whole—

JESS. But like two hours? Four? Dinner and a movie? Four hours?
Five?

JOHN. Oh. I'm not // sure—

JESS. Could I stay here?

...

JOHN. In my
apartment?

JESS. Just while yer gone.
I'd like to stay here.

JOHN. ...Why?

JESS. I won't fuck with yer shit. Promise.

JOHN. But...without me here?

JESS. I just want one night.
I just want something that's mine fer one night.
Even if it's yours.

Say yes.

JOHN. But—

JESS. Because I took off work.
On the night I make most my money fer the week. To live.
So I could be here.
With you.

> *John sees her dress.*
> *The wine.*
> *Her face.*

JOHN. Oh.

JESS. No one's gonna be here, right? This place will just be here.
Warm 'n empty. With no one in it while yer gone.

JOHN. Yeah but—

JESS. Say yes.

JOHN. ...

JESS. ...

JOHN. I don't really...
I
I'm sorry but
I don't
feel comfortable. You here.
Without me.

JESS. Why.

JOHN. I just—

JESS. Why.

JOHN. You've taken some
stuff // before—

JESS. What stuff.

JOHN. It doesn't—

JESS. What.

JOHN. Soap.

I know you took, which—It's fine.
It's just *[soap]*—But—
I would rather be here.
Whenever you are.

That's all.

JESS. I can give it back.

JOHN. It's fine.

   …

Why'd you take it?

   …

JESS. I can give it back.

JOHN. Could we just
Let's just
Shave and a shower.

And I'll pay you overtime,
since you're over time.

Okay?

JESS. Shave and a shower.
Okay.
Yeah.

JOHN. Thanks.

> *An awkwardness and strangeness hangs between them. Something's changed for good.*

Hey at least you'll get to
go home early.
For a change.

JESS. Right.

> *John exits toward the bathroom.*

...

Jess stands a moment...

Right.

...then runs out of the apartment, her coat in her arms.

Eight.

Jess has just run out of John's apartment, humiliated and lost.
It snows around her.
She takes out her cell and makes a call.

The disappointment of an answering machine.
Raw need floods a non-English language. (Italics not in parenthesis indicate words spoken in another language.)

JESS. I was really hoping you'd pick up. *I miss you so much. I wish I could talk to you. (Re: illness.) I wish you were—still you.*
I love you.
I'm sorry. I just—I miss you. I'm sorry. I'm sorry.
I'm sorry.

Bye, *Mommy.*

      She hangs up.
      She looks up and watches the snow falling out the sky.
      Snow.
      Wind.
      Night.
      Jess exits.

Nine, or Epilogue.

Eddie's apartment.
Boxes inside. Snow outside.
Later that night.
Something feels different.

Eddies enters, goes to a box. Rummages through it.

EDDIE. *(To someone offstage.)* It's somewhere in here sorry. Sorry I know it's in here somewhere.

> *He rummages.*

You wanna come in? Warm up a bit while I—

> *He rummages. Sees this person has not budged.*

Or—okay. Or keep enjoyin the view.
Of Bayonne.

> *Jess walks into the doorframe, careful, alert, suspicious. And on the defensive.*
> *She wears a coat. Beneath it, the dress she wore to John's tonight over the warmest sweatpants and winter boots she owns. She does not fully enter yet.*

You can see pretty much the whole rest of the apartment from where yer standin. So that's the tour.
But you can also come in.
If you want.

JESS. Where is she?

EDDIE. Oh.
She kinda comes 'n goes—

JESS. Yer wife kinda comes 'n goes?

EDDIE. We're uh
We're separating so she—

JESS. You said you 'n yer wife live here. That's why // I was even willing to come near here.

EDDIE. We do. We did.

78

JESS. So where is she? She gonna be hidin in the closet? In one a these boxes? Somebody gonna jump out these boxes and like, take my organs— *(Re: door.)* Keep it open.

You really got a wife?

He shows her a picture from his wallet.

Could be yer sister.

EDDIE. It's not.

And anyway, even if it was, wouldn't it calm you down you just met a dude carries around pictures of his—adopted—sister?

JESS. Just sayin, not really a lady's touch in here.

EDDIE. Well neither is that car you were sleepin in. Miss Lady.

You checkin to see if I had money?

JESS. What?

EDDIE. In my wallet.

JESS. No. What? // No, man—

EDDIE. See, this is why people don't help people.

JESS. *(Turning to exit.)* This was a stupid idea—

EDDIE. Just drink some tea at least!

If yer just gonna go back 'n fuckin, sleep in yer car all night—then come in a minute, have some tea.

She stops. Snow falls around her in the door frame.

It's awful outside. And you, out there, in yer icebox of a car.

I woulda invited you in no matter who you were. A man or a—

JESS. Right.

EDDIE. I woulda.

1 A.M. on a Friday night, you don't know who could be out there.

JESS. I've been doin this a few weeks now, I can handle myself.

EDDIE. A few weeks?, you been sleepin in yer—?

JESS. I usually have heat goin. But the battery died.

Where's the—

EDDIE. Found it.

He finds a blanket in one of the boxes. Ani's blanket.

He hesitates
then hands it to Jess.

JESS. Thank you. This is really gonna be—Thanks—helpful. Out there.

She is about to leave—

EDDIE. If you could just—leave it by the door? In the morning? Or whenever yer done // with—

JESS. Yeah, okay.

EDDIE. Appreciate it.

Sentimental.

Jess is about to leave—
then remembers where she's come from and where she's going.
Pauses.

JESS. I'm just gonna warm up for a minute.

EDDIE. Okay.

JESS. That's all.
Then I'm gone.

    ...

EDDIE. I got pizza should still be good. I can heat it.
(Carefully.) I won't…I won't give you money. But I'll feed you.

I knew a lady, not far from here, she died in her car doin what yer doin. She'd keep her car runnin while she was sleepin in it and a gas can in the back in case she ran outta—And one night it tipped over. A lady. Young. 32 or something, 33. They found her in the morning. Suffocated. The fumes.
A stupid thing. Small, stupid things.
A gas can.
And then she—wasn't.

I saw you in yer car and I—I dunno, you never know, y'know?

Jess hasn't moved.
Snow around her.

I got pizza. If you want it.

JESS. What kind?

EDDIE. Plain.

80

JESS. It's good?

EDDIE. From last night.

You gonna come in?

...

JESS. I dunno get the pizza.

...

EDDIE. You gonna steal my shit? While I heat this slice?

JESS. What shit am I gonna steal? 'N put where?

...

...

EDDIE. Don't steal my shit.

> *Eddie exits, to heat a slice. We hear a microwave in the darkness of the apartment.*
>
> *Jess stands—looking around—but always near the door.*
>
> *Eddie returns. The microwave hums in the distance.*

JESS. I work.

EDDIE. Okay.

JESS. I'm not some kinda—just sleepin in a car, okay? // I work.

EDDIE. Okay.

JESS. 'Til 4 A.M. some nights.
At bars, so don't get any ideas.
I woulda usually been workin tonight. Fer most of the night.
I—I wasn't tonight. But I usually woulda.

> *The microwave beeps.*

I'm not some fuckin—just sleeps in a car. I went to school. I work.

EDDIE. You wanna come inside?

JESS. I am inside.

EDDIE. More inside?

JESS. I'm good here.

EDDIE. Okay but the snow is—

JESS. Oh.

EDDIE. I mean, I don't have any nice stuff or anything, *rugs*, that

I'm like, worried about here but—snow's fallin inside.
I don't want you to trip.

JESS. I'm careful.

EDDIE. Okay.

> *She still stands by the door.*
> *Then,*
> *She takes one step closer in.*
> *And closes the door slightly—still keeping it open. Ready.*

Want me to take yer // coat?

JESS. I don't walk into houses, I want you to know that, I also don't just walk into houses.

EDDIE. Yeah of course—

JESS. I'm careful. I sleep during the day—usually—cuz I'm so careful. I arranged my life so I work at night—'til // 4 A.M. some nights—

EDDIE. 'Til 4 A.M. yeah that's late.

JESS. Don't make fuckin fun of me, you ever work all fuckin night?

EDDIE. Yeah. Yes. I have.
Lots of times actually.
Too many.

JESS. …Okay.
Okay so you know.
I sleep at different points in the day, at some point in the day. People leave me alone, mostly. They see someone asleep in their car but it's in the day, the early day, and they kinda leave you alone.
Mostly.

EDDIE. It's cold though.

JESS. Yeah.
Yeah I haven't figured that all out yet. This season.
It is.
It's cold.

> *She sees the past few months of her life in her mind. Tries to*
> *pretend they aren't there.*

It's really fuckin cold.

> *The microwave beeps again. A reminder.*

It's little breaks, y'know? Car. The car. Health stuff, some problems—
that cleans you out fast. Bad luck. Mistakes. Some mistakes. Was
hoppin on couches fer a while but that gets old quick—bein the one
that always needs something. I got old.

EDDIE. Where's yer...?

JESS. I don't have family here, not anymore, in the country.
She got sick 'n went back.
We couldn't afford—Not here.
I've been sendin money but it's—you know—

EDDIE. Yeah.

JESS. Not enough.   EDDIE. Never enough.
So I'm sleepin in her car.
I can send more that way.

We used to live not far from here. So that's where I park.

EDDIE. By my place.

JESS. Yeah.

EDDIE. So we're neighbors.

   ...

She died.

JESS. Yeah I know, the woman in the car—

EDDIE. No. My wife. She died. Last month.
Please don't go.
Or you can go. If you want. But don't. Please.
We can have an arrangement. You can crash every once in a while.
Or
Or you can live here.
We can split the place. This place. I'll pay more. I don't have much,
y'know, money but. I'm outta work now but I'll get employed again.
I just—I need someone here. I just need someone here. With me.
I'm sorry yer a woman.
Not *that* yer a woman but I know that makes this all a little weird.
I keep the lights on now. Every room. All the time.
I would pay fer those! You wouldn't hafta pay fer those.
It's...it's just um...being alone...here is...
I don't know what to do—

The microwave beeps.

JESS. The pizza's…

EDDIE. Yeah.

Yeah okay.

> *This feels to Eddie like a defeat.*
> *But he will still get the slices. Eddie exits.*
>
> *Jess looks around.*
> *She closes the door.*
> *It's instantly warmer.*
>
> *Jess considers.*
>
> *Eddie returns with two slices of pizza on paper towels.*

(Re: paper towels.) Plates were dirty. Didn't wanna make you wait.

> *She sees him. Sees something in him.*
>
> *He sees something too.*
> *In this moment, he doesn't think he'll ever see this person again.*

You want it, um, To-Go? In a bag?

JESS. How much is rent?

EDDIE. Twelve! We can pro-rate it!

JESS. Don't get too excited.

EDDIE. *(He is.)* I'm not!

JESS. Yer not excited I could be livin with you?

EDDIE. I am. I // "would."

JESS. Don't get excited. I'm just askin.

EDDIE. I'm not a weird person either.

JESS. Cool I trust you now.

EDDIE. I don't even go to bars. Not usually. Or stay out late.

JESS. But you were tonight.

EDDIE. But I'm usually not. I'm usually not so I wouldn't have usually even seen you out there, that late, in yer car. This was an unusual thing I did tonight. I was goin to meet someone.

I got stood up actually.

By a—

I was on my way home. And I found you.

84

JESS. Oh you didn't "find" me.

EDDIE. Okay.

JESS. You saw me.
I *let* you see me.

I was just askin. About the rent. Just—to ask.

EDDIE. Sit. Eat.

JESS. I'll stand.

EDDIE. Okay.

>   *He holds out her slice.*

JESS. Take a bite of my pizza.

>   *He does.*
>   *Ta da. Still alive.*
>   *Then he gives her the slice.*
>   *She holds it, unsure whether to eat it.*
>   *Or to stay.*

EDDIE. The poison's gonna take at least an hour so we got some time still to converse.

>   *She stares at him.*
>   *He laughs.*
>   *He laughs at his own joke.*
>   *Maybe he laughs too loud and too long.*
>   *Maybe he becomes devastated at thinking about death, even joking about it, at this moment in his life.*
>   *Maybe he thought he was okay sooner than he really is.*
>
>   *Something happens to a very lonely man here.*

I'm not a weird person.

JESS. I think I'm gonna go.

EDDIE. Do you have tea? Fer the car?

JESS. I don't have any way to make hot water.

EDDIE. I'll give you some. Please don't go.

>   *She puts down the slice somewhere.*

Take the slice.

JESS. That's okay.

EDDIE. What's yer name?

JESS. *(Exiting.)* I'm sorry.

EDDIE. What's yer number?

JESS. No.

EDDIE. *(Approaching her.)* Area code? Did you get a new number recently? What's yer area code?

JESS. I have mace in my bag!

> *He freezes. Hands up.*

EDDIE. …Thank you fer tellin me. Instead of just—

JESS. You don't seem like—
It's just unfortunate that some people have already lived a lot of life before they meet other people.
I'm sorry.

> *Jess goes to the door.*

EDDIE. Just—okay—be careful though, okay?
Stupid things. It can be a small, stupid thing. A blood clot while I was gone on a drive. A tiny vein.
And then she wasn't.

JESS. *(About your wife.)* I'm sorry.
(About leaving.) But…I'm sorry.

EDDIE. Just—be careful.
And—and make sure someone's watchin you, I guess, in y'know… in some kinda way.

JESS. 973.

EDDIE. What?

JESS. Is my area code. 973.

> …

EDDIE. Oh.
Okay.
(Disappointed.) She was 201.

JESS. Thanks fer…trying.

EDDIE. Thanks fer…yeah…you too.

> *Jess exits.*

Eddie takes off his coat.
It slumps or hangs somewhere.

He stands alone in his space a moment.

He goes to the pizza she left.
And he holds it in his hands.

…

Then,
Eddie's phone buzzes
from somewhere within his coat.

He stops.
He turns towards it.
Stands.

…

He fears going to his phone.

…

Then,
the doorknob turns.
He jumps back.

Snow.
Wind.

Come in.

Snow.

Then,
Jess enters.

She has a thermos with her.
She stands with the snow around her.

JESS. I brought coffee. But it's old.

EDDIE. I have pizza.
But
it's cold.

You wanna come in?

She takes off her hat.
And takes one step inside.
Toward Eddie.
He takes one step toward her.
Two people stand together in a fading light.

End of Play

PROPERTY LIST

(Use this space to create props lists for your production)

SOUND EFFECTS
(Use this space to create sound effects lists for your production)

Note on Songs/Recordings, Images, or Other Production Design Elements

Be advised that Dramatists Play Service, Inc., neither holds the rights to nor grants permission to use any songs, recordings, images, or other design elements mentioned in the play. It is the responsibility of the producing theater/organization to obtain permission of the copyright owner(s) for any such use. Additional royalty fees may apply for the right to use copyrighted materials.

For any songs/recordings, images, or other design elements mentioned in the play, works in the public domain may be substituted. It is the producing theater/organization's responsibility to ensure the substituted work is indeed in the public domain. Dramatists Play Service, Inc., cannot advise as to whether or not a song/arrangement/recording, image, or other design element is in the public domain.

NOTES
(Use this space to make notes for your production)